Nightmare Bugs!

Africanized HONEYBEES

By Natalie Humphrey

Gareth Stevens
PUBLISHING

HOT TOPICS

Please visit our website, www.garethstevens.com. For a free color catalog of all our high-quality books, call toll free 1-800-542-2595 or fax 1-877-542-2596.

Library of Congress Cataloging-in-Publication Data

Names: Humphrey, Natalie, author.
Title: Africanized honeybees / Natalie Humphrey.
Description: Buffalo, NY : Gareth Stevens Publishing, [2025] | Series: Nightmare bugs! | Includes bibliographical references and index.
Identifiers: LCCN 2023042335 | ISBN 9781538292068 (library binding) | ISBN 9781538292051 (paperback) | ISBN 9781538292075 (ebook)
Subjects: LCSH: Africanized honeybee–Juvenile literature. | Bees–Juvenile literature. | Introduced organisms–Juvenile literature.
Classification: LCC QL568.A6 H838 2025 | DDC 595.79/9–dc23/eng/20231204
LC record available at https://lccn.loc.gov/2023042335

First Edition

Published in 2025 by
Gareth Stevens Publishing
2544 Clinton St
Buffalo, NY 14224

Copyright © 2025 Gareth Stevens Publishing

Designer: Andrea Davison-Bartolotta
Editor: Natalie Humphrey

Photo credits: Cover Perytskyy/Shutterstock.com; series art (texture) Video_Stock _Production/Shutterstock.com; series art (lines) Hananta S/Shutterstock.com; series art (sign) Mr Doomits/Shutterstock.com; series art (trees) Wilqkuku/Shutterstock.com; p. 5 iStockphoto.com/jamesbenet; p. 7 Pamela Au/Shutterstock.com; p. 9 heckepics/iStockphoto.com; p. 11 (bee) Lian van den Heever/Shutterstock.com; p. 11 (blue on map) File:Spread of Africanized Honey Bees.gif/Wikimedia Commons; p. 11 (map) petch one/Shutterstock.com; p. 13 BlueRingMedia/Shutterstock.com; p. 15 Pamela Au/Shutterstock.com; p. 17 File:Apis mellifera scutellata 1355020.jpg/Wikimedia Commons; p. 19 iStockphoto.com/Kristyna Sindelkova; p. 21 Marieke Peche/Shutterstock.com; p. 22 Kuttelvaserova Stuchelova/Shutterstock.com; p. 23 © Lucy Keith-Diagne/iNaturalist.org; p. 25 Cindy Davey/Shutterstock.com; p. 27 Jeremy Christensen/Shutterstock.com; p. 28 Evelyn Joubert/Shutterstock.com; p. 29 Wirestock Creators/Shutterstock.com; p. 30 (bees) TaniaKitura/Shutterstock.com; p. 30 (stamp) Miloje/Shutterstock.com.

All rights reserved. No part of this book may be reproduced in any form without permission in writing from the publisher, except by a reviewer.

Printed in the United States of America

Some of the images in this book illustrate individuals who are models. The depictions do not imply actual situations or events.

CPSIA compliance information: Batch #CS25GS: For further information contact Gareth Stevens, New York, New York at 1-800-542-2595.

CONTENTS

The Africanized Honeybee. 4

Made by Science. 6

Into the Wild 8

Where Are They Now? 10

What Do They Look Like? 12

How Scary Could They Be? 14

Bee Venom 16

Killer Bees 18

Making Honey 20

Home in the Colony. 22

The Swarm! 26

Staying Safe. 28

Tiny Terrors. 30

For More Information. 31

Glossary. 32

Index 32

The Africanized HONEYBEE

Most honeybees aren't too scary, but Africanized honeybees are like something out of a nightmare! While most bees would rather buzz the other way, Africanized honeybees will chase down anyone who gets too close to their hive. But that's not the only scary thing about these bees!

Terrible Truths
Africanized honeybees are sometimes called killer bees.

Made by SCIENCE

In 1956, Brazilian scientists tried to make a better bee. They **bred** European honeybees with African honeybees. They hoped to make a bee that would make more honey and live better in Brazil's warmer **climate**. Instead, they made a more **aggressive** hybrid bee!

Terrible Truths
A hybrid is the offspring of two animals or plants of different kinds.

Into the WILD

In 1957, African honeybee queens escaped **captivity** in Brazil. A group of European honeybee workers followed the queens. These bees formed groups, or colonies, with other bees in the area.

Terrible Truths

Africanized honeybees will form colonies with both wild honeybees and honeybees raised to produce honey that is sold.

Where Are They NOW?

Since their escape from Brazil, Africanized honeybees have spread through South America, Central America, and eastern Mexico. They are also found in Arizona, California, Nevada, New Mexico, Texas, and Oklahoma. Scientists believe they'll keep spreading through the southern United States!

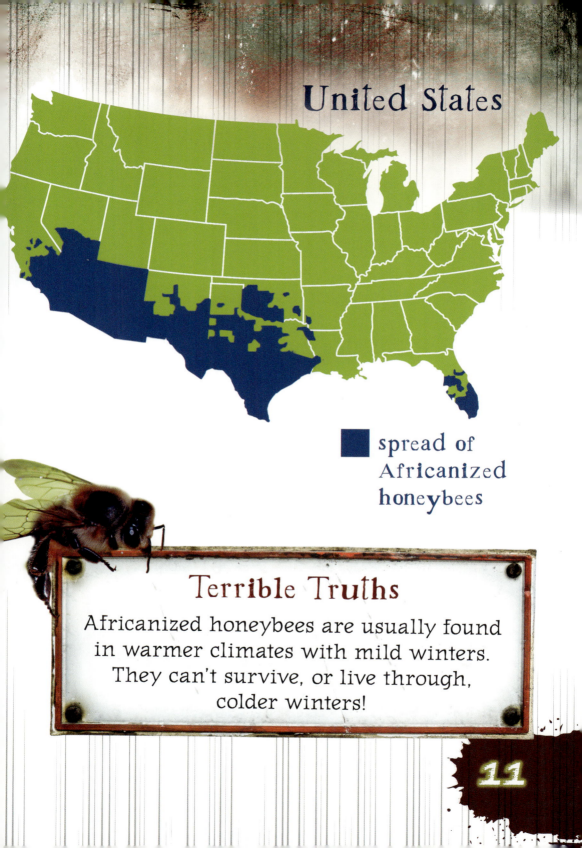

What Do They LOOK LIKE?

Africanized honeybees look very similar to European honeybees. It's even hard for scientists to tell the bees apart! Africanized honeybees are usually about 0.7 inch (19 mm) long. This is a bit smaller than European honeybees. Their bodies are golden yellow with black stripes, just like European honeybees!

A Bee's Body

head

wings

stinger

Terrible Truths

Scientists will often look at a honeybee's **DNA** to find out if it is an Africanized honeybee.

13

How Scary Could THEY BE?

Africanized honeybees are always ready for a fight if they're near their hive. These bees won't just attack predators, they'll attack humans and other bees too! Africanized honeybees are known to chase anyone who gets too close to the colony's hive for long distances.

Terrible Truths
Africanized honeybees can fly as fast as 12 to 15 miles (19 to 24 km) per hour.

Bee VENOM

Getting stung by a bee is always painful. This is because bees have **venom** in their stingers! Bee venom causes a lot of pain and **swelling** around the bee sting. Africanized honeybees have venom just like other bees.

Terrible Truths
One Africanized honeybee's venom isn't any stronger than any other kind of honeybee's venom.

17

Killer BEES

It's not the venom that makes this bee a killer, it's the number of stings! Africanized honeybees attack as a group, and they'll sting more times than European honeybees will. One bee sting might not have a lot of venom, but many stings are enough to kill a person!

Terrible Truths
Since being introdcued in Brazil, Africanized honeybees have caused 1,000 human deaths.

Making HONEY

Africanized honeybees might be scary, but they still pollinate flowers like other honeybees! When a honeybee collects nectar from flowers to make honey, pollen collects in hairs on its body. Then it flies to a new flower, and the pollen is moved from one plant to another.

African honeybee

Terrible Truths

Nectar, or the sweet liquid made by flowering plants, is eaten by honeybees and used to make honey. Honey is used as food for the bees in the colony! Just like other bees, Africanized honeybees make honey.

Home in the COLONY

Africanized honeybee colonies are just like other bee colonies! There are three different kinds of bees: the queen, workers, and drones. The queen bee is the largest female honeybee in the colony and the only one that can lay eggs.

queen   drone   worker

Terrible Truths

Even though queen bees can live up to five years, they aren't usually the queen for that long! Queen bees are often replaced within two years.

Worker bees help to take care of the hive and the colony. Worker bees collect nectar, take care of baby bees, guard the colony, and build the hive. When people get stung by honeybees, it's usually the workers!

Terrible Truths

Drones are the only male bees in the colony. Their only job is to **mate** with the queen to make baby bees! They live for around three months.

The SWARM!

When Africanized honeybees are ready to find a new home, they swarm! Swarming is when a group of honeybees is on the move, following a queen bee. The queen finds an area she'd like to live, and the worker bees start making the hive.

Terrible Truths
A swarm is a large group of insects, or bugs, that usually fly. Africanized honeybees swarm more often than European honeybees.

honeybee swarm

Staying SAFE

Africanized honeybees might be scary, but there are easy ways to keep yourself safe from them. If you spot a small hive, give it a lot of space. If the hive is close to your home, tell an adult!

Terrible Truths

Africanized honeybees might be scary, but **exterminators** can take care of them!

Tiny Terrors
AFRICANIZED HONEYBEES

Size: 0.7 inch (19 mm)

Appearance: golden yellow and black striped bodies

Life span: up to three to six months; queens live up to five years

Where Do They Live? found in South America, Central America, eastern Mexico, and the southwestern United States

Diet: nectar from flowers

Nightmare Fact: They can sense a human or animal from 50 feet (15 m) away!

FOR MORE INFORMATION

BOOKS

Culliford, Amy. *Killer Bees*. New York, NY: Crabtree Publishing Company, 2022.

Peterson, Megan Cooley. *Killer Bees*. Mankato, MN: Black Rabbit Books, 2024.

WEBSITES

A–Z Animals: Africanized Bee
www.a-z-animals.com/animals/africanized-bee-killer-bee/
Find out more facts about Africanized honeybees and where they're found!

Pest World for Kids: Bee Facts for Kids
www.pestworldforkids.org/pest-guide/bees/
Learn more about the different kinds of bees found around the world.

Publisher's note to educators and parents: Our editors have carefully reviewed these websites to ensure that they are suitable for students. Many websites change frequently, however, and we cannot guarantee that a site's future contents will continue to meet our high standards of quality and educational value. Be advised that students should be closely supervised whenever they access the internet.

GLOSSARY

aggressive: Showing a readiness to attack.
breed: To mate two animals with desired qualities in order to produce more like them.
captivity: The state of being caged.
climate: The average weather conditions of a place over a period of time.
DNA: Part of the body that carries genetic information, which gives the instructions for life.
exterminator: Someone who gets rid of pests.
mate: To come together to make babies.
pollinate: To take pollen from one flower, plant, or tree to another.
swell: To cause something to become larger than its usual size.
venom: Something an animal makes in its body that can harm other animals.

INDEX

African honeybees, 6, 8
body, 12, 13, 20, 30
Brazil, 6, 8, 10, 19
colonies, 8, 22
drones, 22, 24
European honeybees, 6, 12, 18, 27
hive, 4, 14, 26, 28
nectar, 20, 21, 24, 30
queen bees, 22, 23, 26
speed, 15
spread, 10
stingers, 13, 16
stings, 16, 18
worker bees, 8, 22, 24, 26